Learn Your ABCs and Numbers 1 2 3

Janet Diana

WestBow Press books may be ordered through booksellers or by contacting:

WestBow Press
A Division of Thomas Nelson & Zondervan
1663 Liberty Drive
Bloomington, IN 47403
www.westbowpress.com
1 (866) 928-1240

ISBN: 978-1-9736-6868-8 (sc)
ISBN: 978-1-9736-6869-5 (e)

Library of Congress Control Number: 2019909147

Print information available on the last page.

WestBow Press rev. date: 8/5/2019

WESTBOW
PRESS®
A DIVISION OF THOMAS NELSON
& ZONDERVAN

This book is dedicated to my mother Dorel, sister Blossom and Cousin Joan-Family is all that matters. Love you lots!!

"Education is the key to success in life and teachers make a lasting impact in the lives of their students." Solomon Ortiz

Learn Your ABCs

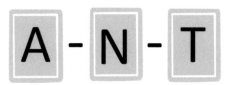

ANT

BANANA

CAR

D - O - G

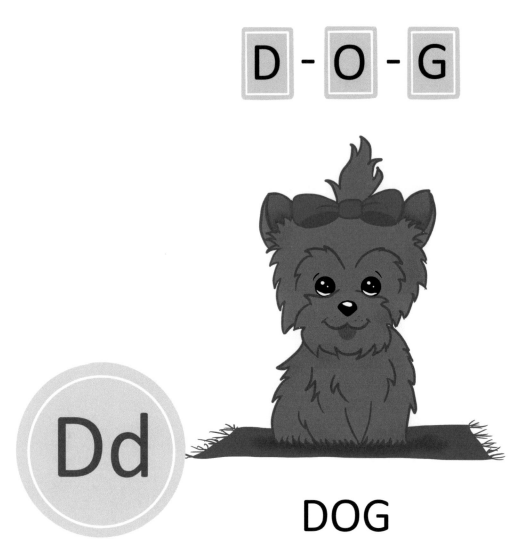

Dd

DOG

E - L - E - P - H - A - N - T

Ee

ELEPHANT

F - O - X

Ff

FOX

G-R-A-P-E-S

GRAPES

H - O - R - S - E

HORSE

I-G-L-O-O

Ii

IGLOO

J - A - C - K

Jj

JACK

K - A - N - G - A - R - O - O

Kk

KANGAROO

L-I-O-N

LION

M-O-T-H-E-R

Mm

MOTHER

N-U-M-B-E-R

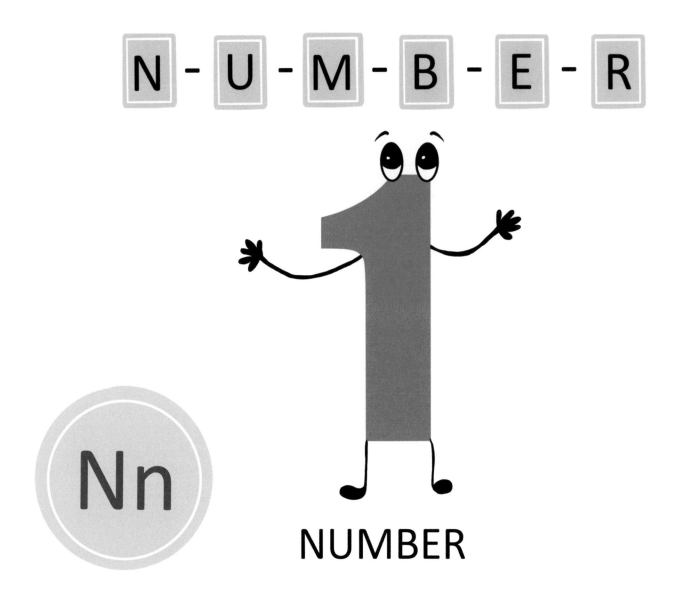

Nn

NUMBER

O-R-A-N-G-E

Oo

ORANGE

P - E - A - R

PEAR

Pp

Q-U-I-L-L

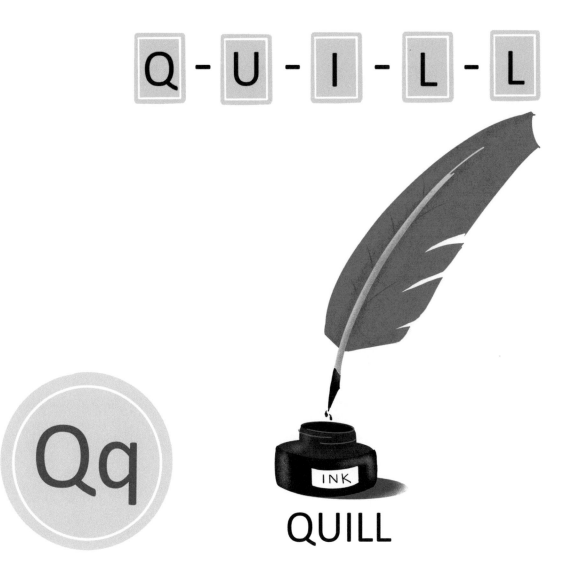

Qq

QUILL

R - A - B - B - I - T

Rr

RABBIT

S -T -A -R -F -I -S -H

Ss

STARFISH

T-U-R-T-L-E

Tt

TURTLE

U -M -B -R -E -L -L -A

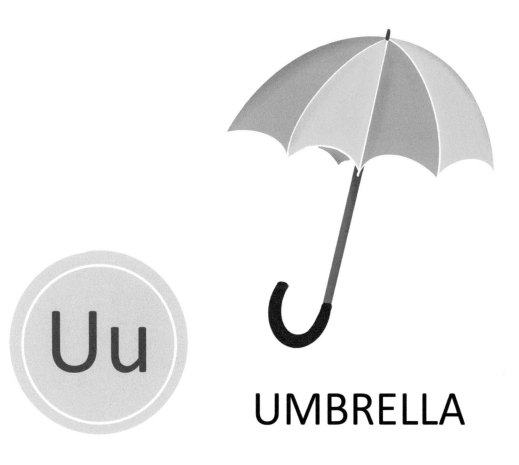

Uu

UMBRELLA

V - A - C - U - U - M

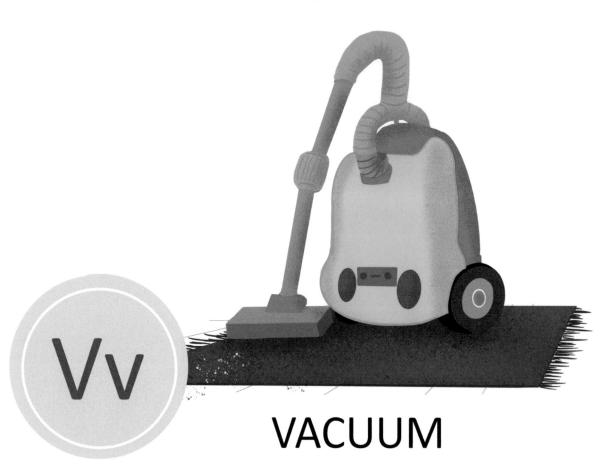

Vv

VACUUM

W - A - L - N - U - T

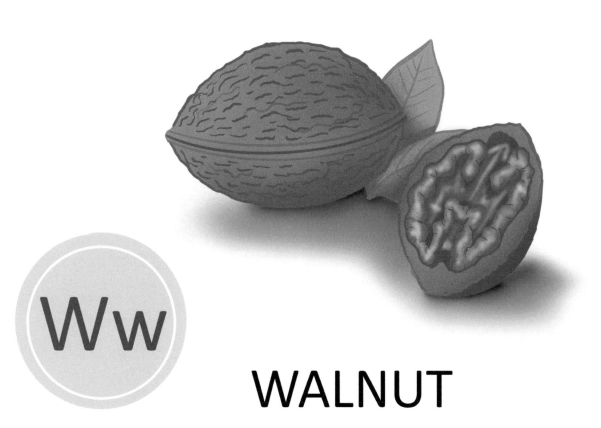

Ww

WALNUT

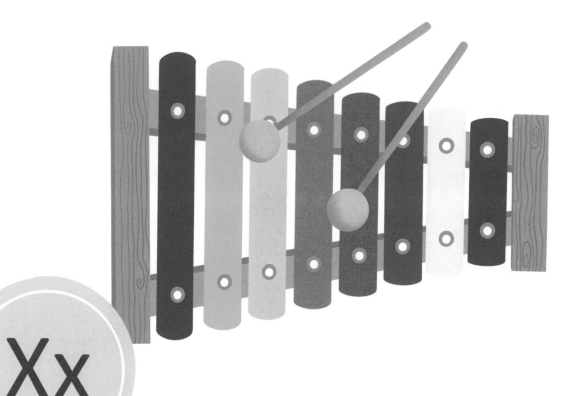

Xx

XYLOPHONE

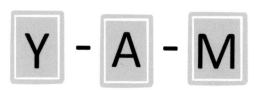

YAM

Z - O - O

ZOO

Learn Your Numbers

1

One

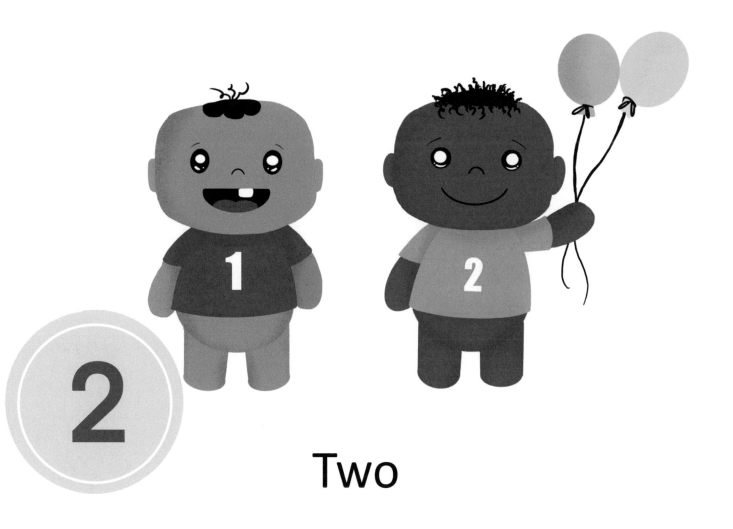

2

Two

3

Three

4

Four

5

Five

6

Six

7

Seven

Eight

9

Nine

Ten

Find the
Numbers

Can you find them?

1 tooth

2 balloons

3 butterflies

4 teeth

5 strings

6 petals

7 stripes

8 hearts

9 bees

10 dots

Printed in the United States
By Bookmasters